RUPERT BROOKE

David Boyle has been writing about new ideas for more than a quarter of a century. He is co-director of the New Weather Institute, a fellow of the New Economics Foundation, has stood for Parliament and is a former independent reviewer for the Cabinet Office. He is the author of *Alan Turing, Scandal* and *Before Enigma,* as well as a range of other historical studies. He lives in the South Downs.

Rupert Brooke
England's last patriot

David Boyle

THE REAL PRESS
www.therealpress.co.uk

Published in 2015 by the Real Press. Kindle edition by Endeavour Press. New print edition 2016. www.therealpress.co.uk
© David Boyle

ISBN (print) 978-1522785668

For Andrew

Contents

If I should die, think only this of me:
That there's some corner of a foreign field
That is forever England. There shall be
In that rich earth a richer dust concealed;
A dust whom England bore, shaped, made aware,
Gave, once, her flowers to love, her ways to roam,
A body of England's, breathing English air,
Washed by the rivers, blest by the suns of home.
And think, this heart, all evil shed away,
A pulse in the eternal mind, no less
Gives somewhere back the thoughts by England
given;
Her sights and sounds; dreams happy as her day;
And laughter, learnt of friends; and gentleness,
In hearts at peace, under an English heaven.

Rupert Brooke, 'The Soldier', 1914

I
Introduction

"It's too wonderful for belief. I had not imagined
Fate could be so benign. I almost suspect her.
Perhaps we shall be held in reserve, out of sight,
on a choppy sea, for two months - yet even that!
But I'm filled with confident and glorious hopes.
I've been looking at the maps. Do you
think perhaps the fort on the Asiatic corner will
want quelling, and we'll land and come at it from
behind, and they'll make a sortie and meet us on
the plains of Troy? It seems to me strategically so
possible. Shall we have a Hospital Base (and
won't you manage it?) on Lesbos? Will Hero's
Tower crumble under the 15" guns? Will the sea
be polyphloisbic and wine-dark and
unvintageable? Shall I loot mosaics from St
Sophia, and Turkish Delight, and carpets? Should
we be a Turning Point in History? Oh God! I've
never been quite so happy in my life, I think. Not
quite so pervasively happy; like a stream flowing

entirely to one end. I suddenly realise that the ambition of my life has been—since I was two—to go on a military expedition against Constantinople. And when I thought I was hungry or sleepy or aching to write a poem— that was what I really, blindly, wanted. This is nonsense. Good-night. I'm very tired with equipping my platoon."
Rupert Brooke, letter to Violet Asquith, 25 February 1915

It is now a century since Rupert Brooke died. For many of those who knew him, and many who did not, the news of his death from blood poisoning on a Greek island during the disastrous Dardanelles campaign that was more than a personal disaster – for him and for them. It was a kind of watershed. It was a moment when the symbol of English youth succumbed to the futility of war.

Brooke had become a romantic talisman for them, of beauty and zest for life. At the time, it seemed that there was something about him that seemed to symbolise what the nation could and should be. He represented a hope for the future among the radicals and conservatives alike. The reality was not quite the same: Brooke was deeply nostalgic, deeply puritanical and he was recovering from a nervous breakdown when he died. He had also become, in the final year of his life, almost the reverse of what he had been. From a convinced socialist, a Fabian member, an atheist and a sceptic, he developed a particular horror of the homosexual coterie who had formed such a high proportion of his previous friends – and he had embraced a self-sacrificial embrace of militarism that tuned perfectly with the prevailing public mood.

Above all, he had become a patriot, welcoming the war for the opportunities it provided for simplifying his romantic life and romanticising the world, describing it – like so many others at the time – as a chance to cleanse himself. His phrase "swimmers into cleanness leaping" has been quoted ever since, not – as he intended it – as a description of the noble sacrifice of youth, but as part of the bundle of delusions that made the First World War possible

His death was filled with as many contradictions as he was. He was an officer in a

3

peculiar unit of soldier-sailors, taking orders direct from Winston Churchill as the First Lord of the Admiralty. He was not killed fighting, but from the after-effects of an infected mosquito bite. The military operation that had involved him was abandoned at the end of the year having cost more than 56,000 lives on each side. His death came, not just on St George's Day – the English national day which also doubled as William Shakespeare's birthday – but the evening before his comrades set sail for the attack that would claim so many lives from so many different nationalities.

It was the moment, if you had to pick one moment, when so many illusions were shattered. He had been the supreme exemplar of British youth. He had been the poet that swept to national prominence at the outbreak of war with his famous sonnet 'The Soldier' – "some corner of a foreign field/That is forever England". He was, in short, the last patriot.

The war poets that preceded him, people like Julian Grenfell or Vera Brittain's fiancé Roland Leighton, wrote about the glory or romance of war, as the more traditional poets left behind, Those that followed him, Owen, Sassoon,

Rosenberg and the others, wrote about the horror or the 'pity' of it. Rupert Brooke saw little of either. We might speculate, but with difficulty, about what he would have written if he had lived. Yet his death meant something to his contemporaries. It was, in some ways, the moment that the youth of England lost its hope.

II

The friends

So many of those who are remembered for their part as foot soldiers and heroes of the First World War were born in the 1880s. It was the generation that grew to adulthood in the early years of the twentieth century, and stamped the century with their new freedom, their unchaperoned relationships, their first experience of speed behind the wheel of motor cars, whizzing down the road at 30 miles an hour.

Those in Rupert Brooke's immediate intellectual circle, rooted in the English upper middle classes, were intensely aware of that freedom, and matched it with a freedom of behaviour, thought and ideas which formed the basis of those for the rest of the century. They experimented with new forms of morality, new kinds of writing, new painting and certainly new poetry. They were the generation who first embraced modernism, or first reacted against it. They were also the generation whose lives were overwhelmed, if they survived, by the experience of the First World War.

Living through into the 1960s and 1970s, they dominated the way we understand these events now. They wrote the stories that emerged, just as they wrote the histories that described it.

Rupert Brooke was one of these. He was born on 3 August 1887. He was brought up at Rugby School, where his father William Parker Brooke was a housemaster. Rugby was the famous pioneering independent school – or 'public school' as they were known – taken over and 'reformed' by Thomas Arnold to re-Christianise the upper classes in the 1830s and 40s. It was known also as the scene for Tom Hughes' novel *Tom Brown's Schooldays*. It was this establishment and this life, hearty, sporty and sexually ambiguous, that shaped the education of Brooke.

His mother had a "loud, harsh voice and an alarming manner", according to Rupert's school friend Geoffrey Keynes, brother of the famous economist John Maynard. "She had little sense of humour and seldom laughed," he said. It was

Rupert's mother who Lytton Strachey nicknamed 'The Ranee' – a kind of female rajah – and who would later block a memoir written about Rupert by his patron and friend Eddie Marsh.

The future author of some of the most anthologised poems of Englishness in the language was brought up with a sense of the heart of England. "It is perpetually June in Warwickshire and always six o'clock on a warm afternoon... There are butterflies all the year around and a full moon every night," he wrote immediately before the outbreak of war in the summer of 1914, which is remembered similarly by the generation who survived as a wonderful, unforgettable summer.

From the start, Rupert displayed a tremendous talent for friendship, and his boyish good looks – his profile and floppy hair – had a devastating effect on a certain kind of men, attracting the attention of his peers and elders alike, perhaps more than women. His prep school friend James Strachey was the younger brother of the great cynic Lytton. "Rupert Brooke – isn't it a romantic name," he wrote to the young Virginia Stephen, later Woolf.

Rupert met Virginia himself in 1899 in St Ives, during the Easter holidays, and played cricket with her on the beach. Later, they would bathe naked in the River Cam outside Cambridge – his friendships so often seemed to involve naked bathing. It was the spirit of the times – free, nature-loving and eminently Edwardian. It was also the spirit of the group of friends he surrounded himself with, and Rupert was perhaps more committed to bare feet, dawn swims and sleeping in the dew than any of them. Virginia was also impressed with his great party piece – to dive naked into the river and emerge with an erection. That was, perhaps, the spirit of the age.

This fey element to Rupert's character made him both and insider and an outsider in the emerging circle of friends who would be gathered together later under the title 'Bloomsbury', with the combined and inter-connected, overwrought mutual relationships involving the brilliance of Maynard Keynes, the genius of Virginia Woolf, the waspish wit of Lytton Strachey and a host of minor artistic characters from Duncan Grant to Frances Partridge. Rupert Brooke was an insider because he was involved as a friend or acquaintance of many of them, but also an outsider. His poetry rejected the modernism they embraced, and by the end of his life he had reacted violently against some of the key figures. They were urban souls, though they might base themselves in the countryside, and he was not, as he said. But he shared their tortured approach to love. His many relationships were painful, difficult, self-flagellating and devastating for both sides. It was this that led to his nervous breakdown in 1912.

It was in some ways a direct result of the prevailing moral climate. King's College, Cambridge, where Brooke became a student in 1906, was the centre of a new moral philosophy inspired by the philosopher G. E. Moore, the prophet of moral autonomy. Maynard Keynes described Moore's philosophy like this:

"It was nothing more than the application of logic and rational analysis to the material presented as sense-data. We entirely repudiated a personal liability on us to obey general rules. This was a very important part of our faith, violently and aggressively held."

"Morality could not be calculated," said Moore. "It had to come from within." It was "exciting, exhilarating, the beginning of a renaissance, the opening of a new heaven and earth," wrote Keynes. "We were the forerunners of a new dispensation; we were not afraid of anything." The truth was to be found by intuition as well as reason. It was at the time a liberating creed, and Brooke certainly felt its influence.

So did his friends. It was also potentially confusing rejection of the combined traditions of morality, handed down by those stiff Victorians from their own stuffy forebears. For Rupert and his circle, this meant working out the complex calculations of how to live afresh every time, and for themselves.

Sigmund Freud was working in Vienna, and pop psychology and strange psychological parlour games were all the rage amongst the Edwardian youth, but there were few if any tools for understanding the violent emotions that first youth generation would feel – no concepts widely available to help them understand the attractions and repulsions that so flung Brooke's soul from side to side (though James Strachey would later be psychoanalysed by Freud himself).

Perhaps most of all, he was influenced by the new political climate. The early years of the century were dominated by a titanic clash of political values in Britain. There were the Liberals, fresh from their 1906 election landslide, battling to force through a raft of measures – including the first old age pensions – through a Conservative House of Lords.

At the same time, there was the rising storm of protests, soon buffeting the government from the Suffragists and their militant sisters the Suffragettes, campaigning to give women the vote. It was a frightening period of unprecedented trade union upheaval, and the threat of civil war in Ireland as the Ulster Unionists – encouraged by the parliamentary Conservatives – talked up the prospects of an armed uprising and mutiny if Ireland was given Home Rule.

Rupert came under the influence of the new Fabians, the technocratic proponents of a middle class revolution, gradual and peaceful, guided by the political equivalent of his terrifying mother, Beatrice Webb.

He was always political. On one occasion, after

the outbreak of the Boer War in 1899, Mrs Brooke was at a rally in Rugby town by the pro-Boers, the Liberal radicals who opposed the war, and was astonished to see her twelve-year-old son at the table with the meeting organisers and ready to speak. One look from her dragged him back. Brooke was a formidable political speaker in later life. He knew how to build a circle of absolutely committed loyalty. Virginia Woolf certainly thought that, if he had lived, he would have been remembered not as a poet but as a politician. We will return to this question at the end of the book.

Brooke became an active member of the Fabians at university, but his loyal following emerged even before his interest in politics, and it always included more than a whiff of sexuality. Brooke was always an ambiguous figure. Like so many others in the all-male public school world, accompanied by fearsome warnings about the Sin of Sodom, Brooke was attracted to a number of school friends, whose names were excised from his collected letters by Geoffrey Keynes, and from the official biography that he presided over.

He was always a romantic figure, both in himself and in his attitudes. He described himself to his friend Erica Cotterill as "washy blue eyes, tow-coloured hair, a habit of doing the wrong thing unintentionally, and a propensity for dying young".

This was the Rupert Brooke who encountered his first poet St John Lucas. Lucas gave him a copy of *De Profundis*, the bitter book-length letter written by Oscar Wilde to his lover and nemesis, Lord Alfred Douglas. On his way back from recuperating in southern Europe in 1905, Mrs Brooke forbade him to stop in Paris, where Lucas was staying, and gave him money to go to the theatre in London instead. He went to see the first production of *Peter Pan*. He adored it and returned many times. It was, he wrote to Keynes, "merely and completely the incarnation of all one's childish dreams".

Brooke has been compared to Peter Pan before – the devastating self-obsession, the failure to grow up, the romanticism. The fatal idea also that "to die would be an awfully big adventure".

Brooke left school in the summer of 1906, after the great Liberal landslide victory in the general election at the beginning of the year. For the next few years, he would meet the people with whom he constructed his life, dived into politics and began suffering from a youthful, poseur's world-weariness. He felt, he told Keynes, "a pale ghost who has lived and can now only dream". His poems always betrayed a horror of the process of ageing. The phrase 'sick with memories' occurs in his first mature poem 'The Beginning':

Some day I shall rise and leave my friends
And seek you again through the world's far
            ends,
You whom I found so fair
(Touch of your hands and smell of your hair!),
My only god in the days that were.
My eager feet shall find you again,
Though the sullen years and the mark of pain
Have changed you wholly; for I shall know
(How could I forget having loved you so?),
In the sad half-light of evening,
The face that was all my sunrising.
So then at the ends of the earth I'll stand

And hold you fiercely by either hand,
And seeing your age and ashen hair
I'll curse the thing that once you were,
Because it is changed and pale and old
(Lips that were scarlet, hair that was gold!),
And I loved you before you were old and wise,
When the flame of youth was strong in your
    eyes,
-- And my heart is sick with memories.
Rupert Brooke, 'The Beginning', 1906

It was an appropriately Keatsian note with which to begin his university career and, that autumn, he arrived at King's College, Cambridge. King's was, at the time, the very heart of G. E. Moore's new morality. Moore was a fellow there and the college was the beating heart of the intellectual hothouse that would spin out Bloomsbury. It would give the world not just the novels of E. M. Forster but Keynesian economics, the hidden Marxism of the 1930s that would lead to betrayal and the secret, elite group of intellectuals who called themselves the Apostles. For Rupert Brooke, it was also a place where he could meet again his old friends Geoffrey Keynes, Hugh Russell-Smith and Denis

Browne. On doorstep of the Provost, M. R. James – author of the most famous ghost stories in the language – he also met Hugh Dalton, his most important political friend and later Chancellor of the Exchequer in Labour's post-war Attlee government. Otherwise, he reacted against Cambridge, as he did later in his poem 'The Old Vicarage, Grantchester'. He described the people he met there as "dull, middle-aged and ugly".

The various different strands of his life were beginning to come together. He was roped in to act the part of Herald in a Greek play by Eumenides. As such, he was glimpsed for the first time by the man who would become his most powerful and energetic patron, Eddie Marsh, the high-flying civil servant who would later hitch his career to the flying coat-tails of Winston Churchill. Drama became one of his main activities in Cambridge.

Then there was politics. His friend Ben Keeling had masterminded the growth of the Fabian Society in Cambridge, and he was introduced by Dalton to their treasurer, Amber Reeves, shortly to become the mistress of the Fabians' pet seducer, the great propagandist of scientific rationalism, H.

G. Wells. Brooke held back for a while. "I'm not your sort of socialist," he told Dalton. "I'm a William Morris sort of socialist."

This was revealing. Morris had split the forces of socialism in the 1880s and his utopian romance *News from Nowhere* (1890) had painted a very different future than the ones promoted either by the Marxists or the dullest Fabians. It was an agrarian future without money, and without urban squalor, based on craft, art and a kind of medieval idealised society of equality and beauty. It explains a little more about Brooke, at least at this formative period of his life, where he was just discovering the bucolic pursuit of nature – naked swimming. This was his emerging creed, encouraged by two new friends from the progressive boarding school Bedales, Justin Brooke and Jacques Raverat.

Brooke had also developed a friendship with the Catholic controversialist Hilaire Belloc, who was certainly no socialist, but represented the twentieth century version of Morris' ideal medievalism and Back to the Land politics. Belloc dined in his rooms in King's. It was another clue to the kind of politics Brooke would come to represent. Belloc shared the kind of romantic view of English history, and was still a Liberal MP but was rapidly developing the kind of critique of the economic system that would drive him out of the Liberal Party. The careers of both men were boosted by the outbreak of war in 1914.

Brooke also began to develop a veneer of protective cynicism, what E. M. Forster – another gay admirer from King's – called a "hatred of slosh". This was the necessary defence developed by the attractive against the attracted. It seeped into his letters. They were light, arch, cynical, funny and dishonest. Perhaps they had to be.

Then there were the Apostles. This was a secret society with a record, founded in 1820, and meeting every Saturday at tea in Trinity College to eat anchovies on toast. Moore was a member. So were two of the elder brothers of Rupert's friends, Maynard Keynes and Lytton Strachey. Lytton's brother James was a member too, and desperate to get Brooke elected, hoping perhaps to lure him finally into bed.

Brooke's own sexuality was still confused. Nigel Jones, author of the best biography of him, puts it like this:

"Although he would never be able to conduct a full, mature heterosexual relationship, and his emotions would stay mired in an adolescent swamp, his yearning to prove himself a lover of women would be as much part of his make up as his early homo-eroticism."

This was the story of the rest of his emotional life. But Brooke was no callous seducer. He suffered along with those he loved as their lives became intertwined, and one of these was a wealthy orphan called Ka (Katherine) Cox, who took over from Amber Reeves as treasurer of the Cambridge Fabians. The closest circle of his women friends, who would dominate his emotional life, were coming together, originally through his love of the theatre. Through the Marlow Dramatic Society, he also met Frances and Gwen Darwin, granddaughters of the founder of evolutionary science. Ka Cox was helping with the set design

The other great friends in his emerging circle were the younger two of the four daughters of the Fabian colonial administrator Sir Sydney Olivier, Margery, Daphne, Bryn and Noel. He sat opposite the fifteen-year-old Noel at dinner in Ben Keeling's rooms in Trinity College and fell for her immediately. The Olivier daughters lived in the Surrey Hills, near Box Hill, and were much given to night-time secret expeditions in the woods around their home at Limpsfield Chart. It was to be an important circle of friends for English culture, and their lives interacted for decades. Gwen Darwin married Jacques Raveret, after Ka Cax turned him down. She later wrote an evocative childhood memoir called *Period Piece* (1952).

It was hard to hold all this together with socialism, studying texts at the Fabian summer school while James Strachey continued his attempts to wheedle his way into Rupert's bed. There were long midnight conversations and long walks, and early morning bathing. In fact, youthful friendship became a kind of fetish for them, and especially for Brooke. He was always deeply suspicious of marriage as the cause of aging, dullness and disillusion. He found it hard to forgive his friends Francis Cornford and Frances Darwin for marrying, though they became an important source of stability in his life. Later on, he wrote a poem imagining Menelaus and Helen as an elderly couple, which ended:

"So Menelaus nagged; and Helen cried
And Paris slept on by Scamander side."

But despite his world-weariness, perhaps partly because of the quest for eternal youth, Brooke's obvious zest for life was infectious. He was no natural politician, and certainly not a natural Fabian, with their tables and utilitarian earnestness. There are only three good things in the world, he told Hugh Dalton: "One is to read poetry, another is to write poetry and the best of all is to live poetry."

He was pretending he wasn't, but he was now at least writing poetry. There were those who would later claim he was, in some ways, also living it. One of these was his admirer and friend, Eddie Marsh, another member of the Apostles, now at the Colonial Office where Churchill was a junior minister. He invited Rupert to breakfast and Brooke read one of these new poems to him. It summed up his current approach to life, nostalgic, romantic and slightly morbid. It was called 'Day that I have loved'.

"Tenderly, day that I have loved, I close your
  eyes,
And smooth your quiet brow, and fold your thin
  Dead hands.
The grey veils of the half-light deepen; colour
  dies.
I bear you, a light burden, to the shrouded
  sands,..."

"There was something dateless in his beauty which makes it easy to picture him in other centuries, yet always in England," wrote his friend Frances Cornford later. Despite his politics, his atheism and his cynical modernism, it is primarily as a representative of English poetry and an expression of Englishness that he is remembered now. That is partly to do with the huge success of his anthologised and much-quoted poem 'The Old Vicarage, Grantchester'.

His connection with Grantchester began when he started to look for rooms in the village in 1909, as his tripos date approached. He wanted somewhere quieter where he could revise. He had discovered the village for himself, two miles out of

Cambridge, on walks with Geoffrey Keynes. It already had its link with romantic poetry: Byron – a great swimming pioneer, after all – had bathed there. He found a home there, initially in a house called the Orchard, including two bedrooms and a ground floor sitting room, with free use of the garden. It cost him 30 shillings a week.

Rupert was busily becoming Rupert Brooke. He was already obsessed with Noel Olivier, and had begun a long, fraught correspondence with her. She had a propensity for douching him with cold water. "No doubt you have a tremendous capacity for enjoyment," she replied to one of his rapturous letters. "Only I wish you wouldn't talk of nature in that foolish and innocent tone of voice."

Brooke was the prototype of the type of varsity student which went to seed in Sebastian Flyte a generation later. He wept, used lines from Barrie's *Peter Pan*, wore striped blazers and loose shirts. It was a compelling pose. Brooke was introduced to the great novelist Henry James, who was told he was a poet, but not a good one. "Well, I must say, I am RELIEVED," replied James. "For, with THAT appearance, if he had also talent it would be too unfair". Henry James' last published writing was a tribute to Brooke in 1916.

Returning from an idyllic holiday in Switzerland, Brooke set out the case for his 'Peter Pan' approach to life. He and his friends promised each other they would meet at Basle Station on 1 May 1933:

"We'll be children seventy years, instead of seven. We'll *live* Romance not *talk* of it. We'll show the grey, unbelieving age, we'll teach the whole damn World, that there's a better Heaven than the pale serene Anglican windless harmonium-buzzing Eternity of the Christians, a Heaven in Time, now and for ever, ending for each, staying for all, a Heaven of Laughter and Bodies and Flowers and Love and People and Sun and Wind, in the only place we know or care for ON EARTH."

During one of these pagan camps, in a similarly pantheistic mood, this time in the New Forest, Noel Olivier agreed that they could be secretly engaged, though she was still at school. It was the high point of the romantic, outdoor circle of friends. After the secret engagement, he decamped for the first time to the Old Vicarage, Grantchester. He was eventually to move there more permanently after the locals complained to the landlords of the Orchard about too many young people running around in bare feet.

By now, Rupert was working as hard as he could on writing poems. "Have you seen Rupert's notebooks," remarked Jacques Raverat, "with all the first drafts of sonnets with blanks left for the Oh God's?" You can see his style beginning to emerge, short verses often sonnets which manage to include a mixture of frustrated romanticism and bodily disgust, and often with a bite at the end, as in 'The Hill':

Breathless, we flung us on the windy hill,
Laughed in the sun, and kissed the lovely grass.
You said, "Through glory and ecstasy we pass;
Wind, sun, and earth remain, the birds sing
    still,
When we are old, are old. . . ." "And when we
    die
All's over that is ours; and life burns on
Through other lovers, other lips," said I,
- "Heart of my heart, our heaven is now, is

won!"

"We are Earth's best, that learnt her lesson
here.

Life is our cry. We have kept the faith!" we said;
 "We shall go down with unreluctant tread

Rose-crowned into the darkness!" . . . Proud we
were,

And laughed, that had such brave true things to
say.

- And then you suddenly cried, and turned
away.

Rupert Brooke, 'The Hill', 1910

"I've never seen you 'cry & turn away'," he wrote to
Noel at boarding school, inevitably also Bedales,
the educational arm of the Fabian Society.

The country was now in uproar after David
Lloyd George's People's Budget, attempting to
introduce old age pensions, now blocked by the
built-in Conservative majority in the House of
Lords. Prime Minister H. H. Asquith was forced to
call a general election to fulfil the King's promise
to create the peers to force the budget through.
Brooke was busy helping the Labour Party fight
the election. But it was romance that really

grabbed Brooke.

On holiday, as so often, with his friends in Lulworth Cove in Dorset, Brooke found his feelings shifting towards the more reliable and comforting presence of Ka Cox, and confessed this in a meeting with Noel Olivier before heading off to Germany, writing long, agonised letters to both of them from Munich. Yet it was paradoxically in Munich that he met the woman with whom he enjoyed his first heterosexual love affair, a Belgian sculptor called Elisabeth van Rysselberghe.

Like most of Brooke's intimate relationships, this was an on-off, push-pull affair, full of passion mixed with self-disgust and agonising indecision. He kept Elisabeth secret from his other friends, except possibly Eddie Marsh, and particularly from his fearsome mother, who regarded foreign women with almost as much horror as she regarded gay men.

Brooke is still regarded as a sexually ambiguous figure, and he was. Yet he was first and foremost rather prudish, worrying about bodily functions just as he worried about growing old. He was the quintessential Jungian 'flying boy', rejecting the ties of reality or adult life or commitment, leaping from passion to passion, leaving destruction in his wake. It also seems likely that, despite the gay fumblings his generation went through at boarding school, he only had homosexual sex just once, with his friend Denham Russell-Smith. A letter describing it after Denham died suddenly, in graphic and absolutely honest detail – with none of his usual frothy humour and insincerity – was found in the Berg Collection in the New York Public Library in the 1960s, and therefore escaped the censorious destruction of Geoffrey Keynes.

III

The poet

The summer of 1911 was the last of this idyllic period in Brooke's life. He spent it at the Old Vicarage, where he was in the habit of sleeping on the lawn, with dew in his hair, woken by birds and insects before heading off for his morning swim in the River Cam. It was here that he made friends again with the lynchpin of the Bloomsbury world, Virginia Stephen, shortly to marry Leonard Woolf. She was 29. Bertrand Russell, nearly a generation older, encountered the same set-up. "Young people nowadays are odd," he wrote. "Christian names and great familiarity, rendered easy by a complete freedom from passion on the side of the men." It was a blueprint for the way young people would behave for the rest of the century.

"How many people can one love," he asked Ka. "How many people should one love? What is love? If I love a 6pm, do I therefore love at 7?" These are good questions, but they were becoming agonising ones for Brooke and his closest friends, especially as Elisabeth was in London and he was also meeting her at the National Gallery.

He was now writing passionate and indecisive letters to Ka and simultaneously carrying on flirtations and making assignations with both Olivier sisters, Bryn and Noel. It became clear in 2000, when his letters to an art student called Phyllis Gardner were discovered in a locked box in the British Library, that he was also sleeping with her. The letters had been locked away by Phyllis's sister because their affair was regarded as having ended so cruelly, but they reveal another edge to Brooke's rapidly complicating passionate life. "I remember every inch of you lying here in that strange light," he had written to her. It was a further emotional complication.

His habit of mild dishonesty and close protection complicated matters further. As he wrote later: "If I love a person & say nothing, I'm fairly safe, but if I tell them I deliver myself bound into their hands". But with so many friends now caught in that net, something had to give.

Also in 1911, Brooke became a published poet. His book *Poems* came out to good reviews, including one by his new friend, the critic Edward Thomas (Thomas had not yet started writing poetry himself). "Copies should be bought by everyone over forty who has ever been under forty," wrote Thomas in the *Daily Chronicle*. "It will be a revelation. Also, if they live yet a little longer, they may see Mr Rupert Brooke a poet. He will not be a little one."

Once again, Brooke was regarded, rather as he regarded himself, as a spokesperson for youth. But the strands of this gilded youth were beginning to unravel and now the crisis struck. Unsure whether to commit to Rupert, Ka Cox embarked on an affair with a notorious womaniser, Henry Lamb. Tortured by jealousy, Rupert begged her to marry him.

By the dawn of 1912, it was clear that Brooke was suffering from some kind of breakdown and was under the care of Harley Street doctors. Brooke found himself veering even more violently between passion and despair, increasingly blaming Lytton Strachey – Lamb's friend – for pulling the strings in this new relationship. Brooke persuaded Ka into his own bed with him and then allowed his prudery to overcome him and he turned against her. There is some suggestion that she became pregnant but suffered a miscarriage. Later, he described himself in letters to Ka, from the French Riviera where he had been sent to recover, as "half mad".

The nervous collapse marked the big crisis in Brooke's life. It involved the unravelling of his close circle of friends and his determination to gear himself up as a poet. It meant fewer poems as he recovered, exile from England for the same reason, but also one of his best-known poems: 'The Old Vicarage, Grantchester', nostalgic, tongue-in-cheek, exuberant and quotable:

"Ah God! to see the branches stir
Across the moon at Grantchester!
To smell the thrilling-sweet and rotten
Unforgettable, unforgotten
River-smell, and hear the breeze
Sobbing in the little trees."

Right through until the famous couplet that sums up a particular kind of English nostalgia:

"Deep meadows yet, for to forget
The lies, and truths, and pain? . . . oh! yet
Stands the Church clock at ten to three?
And is there honey still for tea?"

The lies, truths and pain were still there, even in the Cambridgeshire Garden of Eden. But this exile from his friends led to a shift in his direction. It meant new, rather better connected connections and a bitter resentment of some of his old ones. The key friendship at this time was with Eddie Marsh. Marsh was now with Churchill at the Admiralty and his flat at Raymond Buildings in Gray's Inn became a London home for Brooke as he found his feet in poetry circles in the capital.

This was also one of the great moments and places to be writing poetry. The seeds of the continental movements were emerging in England, modernism from France and futurism from Italy. A prodigious generation of English artists was emerging, from Stanley Spencer, Paul and John Nash, Mark Gertler, all in their own way redefining Englishness, rather as Brooke was doing. The American Ezra Pound was stirring up excitement. Edward Thomas was about to forge his historic friendship with Robert Frost that would catapult him into writing poetry. And above them all, the previous generation of poets – W. B. Yeats and John Masefield – were attracting attention and excitement (it was Yeats who called Brooke the "handsomest man in England").

Marsh and Brooke together came up with the idea of a volume of new poetry that could capture this poetry scene. It was they who decided to call it 'Georgian Poetry' after the new king, George V. Georgian poetry came to stand for something pre-war, and was swept aside by the new post-war generation, but it was always broader than the poetry represented by Brooke and Thomas – clear, bucolic, nostalgic and very obviously English, all those attributes the new international style was not. When the first volume appeared at the end of 1912, it also included a range of poets that are not, by any means, Georgian, including Masefield, G. K. Chesterton and D. H. Lawrence.

Eddie Marsh's introduction explained the thinking: "This volume is issued in the belief that English poetry is now once again putting on a new strength and beauty". The first edition sold out straight away, and Marsh carried on producing new editions up to 1922, by which time modernism had conquered all.

Involvement with Marsh also brought Brooke into contact with a whole new circle of friends, poets like Wilfred Gibson, Walter de la Mare and Lascelles Abercrombie, but also in the political world, around the embattled Liberal government. Through Marsh, he met Churchill and found himself soon a member of the close circle of young friends around the Asquith family, a regular visitor to 10 Downing Street.

"Rupert holds such dreadfully conventional views nowadays," wrote Bryn Olivier. He didn't go to her wedding with Hugh Popham, but wrote to her: "We're all twenty-five, and we've done so little – this isn't cheering or polite to an almost married lady. But I wanted to explain my mood."

As he settled into his new life, his rage at his old world began to grow increasingly bitter. He read a paper to the Apostles rejecting the moral philosophy of G. E. Moore. 'Goodness' was the most important quality anyone could possess, he said – it was all a matter of what he called "moral taste". He began describing Bloomsbury as one of the "pestilential" parts of London.

He may not have turned his back on the Fabians, but he was still flirting with Belloc's ideas (Belloc had founded the movement known as Distributism that hear with his book *The Servile State*). He visited one of the most peculiar Distributists, the sculptor Eric Gill – then involved not just with sex with his own daughters but also with his dogs. Gill was not impressed with Brooke. Brooke was also at the first of the famous debates between Distributists and Fabians, this time between Belloc and Bernard Shaw in the Queen's Hall in London. He ran into Noel Olivier there and they snubbed each other.

Like Belloc and Chesterton, Brooke was vitriolic about the role of Rufas Isaacs, made Lord Chief Justice despite his involvement in the Marconi insider dealing affair. It is not at all clear what his politics was at this time, nominally a member of the Fabian Society, attracted by Belloc and his fearsome denunciations, but increasingly involved on a personal level with the children of the Prime Minister.

It was with Eddie Marsh that he first met the lynchpin of his new life, the actress Cathleen Nesbitt, who he now bombarded with passionate letters. She revealed as an old lady (she lived until 1982) that, although they regarded themselves as engaged, they never had sex with each other. Brooke was evidently being careful not to make the same mistake as he did with Ka Cox.

But Brooke was still transforming his life. He had decided, like Robert Louis Stevenson and Hilaire Belloc, to have a romantic tour of the USA followed (at least like Stevenson) by a trip to the South Seas. He set sail from Liverpool in May 1913. There was nobody to see him off at the quayside, so he tipped a passing boy to do it. He wrote another tongue-in-cheek verse about who he missed:

"Would God I were eating plover's eggs,
 And drinking dry champagne,
With the Bernard Shaws, Mr and Mrs
Masefield, Lady Horner, Neil Primrose,
Raleigh, the Right Honourable Augustine
Birrell, Eddie, six or seven Asquiths, and
Felicity Tree,

In Downing Street again."

It was hardly such an obscure life after all. But in Tahiti, where he stayed for some time, he seems to have enjoyed one of the only steady affairs of his life with a woman called Taatamata. After he left, to go home the following year, she wrote him a letter in broken English explaining that she was pregnant. This went down with the liner *Empress of Ireland*, was retrieved some months later and reached Brooke immediately before his death.

The evidence is that Taatamata had a daughter, who herself died childless around 1990. But by the time he received the letter, war had broken out and he was no longer free to act, even if he had wanted to.

IV

The soldier

Brooke arrived back in London on 6 June 1914 to be met at the station in the early hours of the morning by Eddie Marsh, Cathleen and his old school friend Denis Browne, now a composer and music critic. At a supper party at Marsh's flat shortly afterwards, his host pulled out some of his most diverse and brilliant contacts in honour of the returning hero. Here were the artists Duncan Grant and Mark Gertler, the politician Duff Cooper, the novelist Hugh Walpole. Brooke performed a Hawaiian siva-siva dance in Gray's Inn Fields afterwards to entertain them.

There followed a glittering array of the literary and famous, with Marsh by his side – lunches with J. M. Barrie and Henry James. Tea with Stanley Spencer. Evenings with the great theatrical manager Gerald du Maurier (Mr Darling and Captain Hook in *Peter Pan*), while he carried on denouncing the corruption of London in letters to his remaining old friends. He cut Lytton Strachey dead in the foyer of the Drury Lane Theatre. At the same time, he was carrying on a new affair, conducted at Raymond Buildings with Lady Eileen Wellesley, great-granddaughter of the Duke of Wellington.

As the war clouds began to gather during the summer, Brooke began to see more of Marsh's boss. At dinner at 10 Downing Street in July, Churchill offered to get Brooke a commission. But he was still undecided about exactly what to do as the countdown to war began. "If fighting starts I shall have to enlist or go as a correspondent, I don't know," he wrote to Stanley Spencer. "It will be Hell to be in it and Hell to be out if it. At present, I'm so depressed about the war, that I can't talk, think or write coherently."

On 4 August, the day war was declared, he had set off to Norfolk to visit the Cornfords, dreaming of premonitions of disaster. The news of war finally filtered through to their remote village the following day. Back in London in the following weeks, he tried to become a war correspondent, but there was no interest. Then he tried seriously enlisting with a commission and went to Rugby to break the news to his mother.

It was soon clear to Marsh that Churchill would have to deal with the surplus volunteers the Admiralty had received for the navy, and that he would do so by forging a whole new unit called the Royal Naval Division. It would include the Royal Marines and the Royal Naval Reserve and a whole new department of the navy formed especially to fight on land. Did Brooke really want that commission? He told Brooke that the new unit was already drilling at Crystal Palace and confided that Churchill had a plan to use it to hold the Channel ports if the German advance broke through.

Brooke bowed to the inevitable. He was commissioned as a sub-lieutenant in Anson Battalion, in charge of D company 15th platoon, mainly re-designated naval stokers from Northumberland, Scotland and Ireland. Energetic and resourceful, Churchill was close to the Asquiths and particularly close to Asquith's daughter Violet, who is said to have thrown herself from a cliff in despair when she heard about his forthcoming marriage to Clementine. Because of this relationship, there was a natural tendency to gravitate towards the Royal Naval Division among Violet's friends, which included not just Brooke, but his old friend Denis Browne, the composer Clegg Kelly and the scholar Patrick Shaw-Stewart. Violet's brother Arthur Asquith, known as Oc, also joined. She made close friends also with another RND officer, Bernard Freyberg, a New Zealander and destined to be a senior commander in World War II.

All these friends gathered for formal training at Betteshanger in Kent in September. Then, in the early hours of 4 October 1914, still feeling feverish from their typhoid inoculations, they were woken and told to march to Dover carrying their full equipment. Churchill's plan was being put urgently into action.

In Dover, they found they were getting straight on a ship and heading for Dunkirk. Brooke assumed, along with his colleagues, that in Dunkirk they would spend the next month "quietly training". Not a bit of it. To their consternation, they were told that they were going straight for Antwerp, then under siege by the advancing German army, and that they must be prepared for the train to be attacked.

In those desperate first few weeks of the First World War, Antwerp had assumed an enormous significance. The embattled Belgian government was based there. It straddled the road to the Channel ports, and its loss could have meant that the British Expeditionary Force could have been surrounded, cut off from home, as it so nearly was in 1940. Back in September, Churchill had been asked by the War Office, to send a force to Dunkirk and confuse the Germans about allied intentions. He agreed and sent 50 buses from London to make sure they were doubly conspicuous, to confuse German intelligence even further.

While this was happening, the advancing German army had been thrown back at the Battle of the Marne. A frustrated Kaiser ordered that the Channel ports should be taken, and in front of them stood Antwerp. The bombardment of the city began at the end of September. Within days, the Belgian government began to leave the city for Ostend. Churchill was recalled on his way to Dover, and taken straight to meet the Foreign Secretary and the First Sea Lord – still Prince

Louis of Battenberg before he was forced from office because of his German name. They showed him a telegram from the Belgians predicting that Antwerp could hold out for only five days. They asked Churchill for help, which he was delighted to give. Lord Kitchener, the Secretary of State for War, asked him to go in person, and he was soon there, directing the defence of Antwerp. Violet Asquith takes up the story:

"I prided myself on an intimate understanding of Winston and had usually been able to explain his actions to myself though not always to others, but he now took a step which staggered me. On October 5, he telegraphed to my father offering to resign his office and undertake the command of the relieving and defensive forces assigned to Antwerp."

But Antwerp was already in a desperate situation. The problem for the arriving Royal Naval Division was not just that their training had barely begun. They also had no medical supplies. The officers had not been given any ammunition for their revolvers, and many of the men had not yet been taught to fire a rifle or dig a trench. It was a typical British military muddle and came hot in the heels of the desperation of the Battle of Mons, when cooks and other non-combatants had been flung into the front line to stop the enemy advance.

Brooke and his friends arrived in Antwerp without incident and were cheered through the streets. They must have been a strange sight, what Violet Asquith called later "this strange amalgam of stokers, sailors, scholars and musicians". They found a deserted castle garden and snatched a few hours sleep before two shells landed nearby. "The rather dirty and wild-looking sailors trudged," Brooke wrote to Violet, "over lawns, through orchards and across pleasaunces. Little pools glimmered through the trees and deserted foundations and round corners one saw, faintly. occasional Cupids or Venuses – a scattered company of rather bad statues – gleaming quietly."

The following morning, marching towards the sound of gunfire, they relieved the exhausted Belgians. Brooke came under fire for the first time and found he had survived it with his dignity intact. "It's queer to see the people who do break under the strain of danger and responsibility," he wrote. "It's always the rotten ones. Highly sensitive people don't, queerly enough". It also became clear that their luggage had been destroyed by a shell.

Even so, they had arrived too late and, shortly afterwards, the order was given for a general withdrawal. That meant 25 miles on foot, across the River Scheldt, alongside thousands of Belgian civilians escaping, weeping or sleeping as they walked, terrified of the rumours of German 'frightfulness'. Nor was their retreat helped by their battalion commander George Cornwallis West, also now Churchill's father-in-law, who lost their only street map of Antwerp and kept asking passers-by if they had one.

Afterwards, Brooke felt he had witnessed one of the great crimes of human history. It was this experience, along with his great changes of heart following his nervous breakdown only two years before, which led him to embrace the war with such fervent enthusiasm. His biographer Nigel Jones wrote:

"During the long march, Brooke saw many strange and terrible sights – railway stations with their tracks torn up; London buses rushed over to transport troops with their adverts and indicator boards intact; broken-down carts full of hopeless humanity awaiting the Germans – but the most profound change of all was the transformation going on within him – from doubter to passionate warrior; from light-hearted curiosity to furious duty; from cynical lightweight to earnest and deadly serious patriot..."

By October 9, Brooke was back in London in his stained clothes, reporting via Marsh directly to Churchill, and was relaxing in Marsh's flat in Raymond Buildings.

We can look back a little cynically about attitudes like the 'passionate warrior' described by Nigel Jones, because – unlike Brooke - we knew what was to happen next. We know about poison gas, the *Lusitania* and the Somme and Passchendaele and we tend to see the war through the horrors described by the next generation of war poets. But Brooke did not live to see them

Also, popular understanding of the war has now often forgotten the humanitarian outrage that the invasion of Belgium caused in the UK, and we can maybe learn a little of it from Lloyd George's impassioned speech, the equivalent of a statement of British war aims, outlined at the Queen's Hall on 19 September 1914:

"Belgium has been treated brutally. How brutally we shall not yet know. We already know too much. But what had she done? Had she sent an ultimatum to Germany? Had she challenged Germany? Was she preparing to make war on Germany? Had she inflicted any wrong upon Germany which the Kaiser was bound to redress? She was one of the most un-offending little countries in Europe. There she was — peaceable, industrious, thrifty, hard-working, giving offence to no one. And her cornfields have been trampled, her villages have been burnt, her art treasures have been destroyed, her men have been slaughtered — yes, and her women and children too.

Hundreds and thousands of her people, their neat, comfortable little homes burnt to the dust, are wandering homeless in their own land. What was their crime? Their crime was that they trusted to the word of a Prussian King."

This is a speech that retains its power to move. It explains something of why people rallied to the flag and volunteered in such numbers, and amidst such enthusiasm. We also have to remember that some of the stories of atrocities committed in Belgium on the civilian population turned out to be true.

Brooke remarked that the misery of the Belgian civilians he had seen on the retreat from Antwerp, with their belongings piled high on carts, was unnecessary. The German policy of active terror to the civilians had not been put into effect in the cities. But nobody knew, and the horrifying way civilians had been treated in the countryside was all too fresh. More than anything else, this was what had brought public opinion round to such enthusiastic support for the war. We forget now, since the First World War came so close to unraveling civilisation once and for all, that the British at least regarded the war as a necessary sacrifice to save civilization – at least at the beginning. This was the serious mood that gripped Brooke on his return from Belgium. Nothing seemed more important, and he began to feel impatient with any of his friends who felt otherwise – and impatient even with Cathleen for wanting to carry on acting.

But this was not a blind embrace of glory. It was also a hard-headed understanding of the personal consequences for him. "When they told us at Dunkirk that we were all going to be killed in Antwerp, if not on the way there, I didn't think much (as I'd expected) what a damned fool I was not to have written more and done various things better, and been less selfish," he wrote to his friend Rosalind Murray, by then married to the historian Arnold Toynbee. "I merely thought what Hell it is that I shan't have any children – any sons."

Ironically, of course, he not yet received the delayed letter from Taatamata on Tahiti with the news that his daughter was on the way.

There followed a reshuffling for most of his

friends, and he and they and Freyberg moved to Hood Battalion. He spent Christmas 1914 looking after drunken stokers, and drafting the five war sonnets that would make him famous. They were the result of inspiration reciting Donne sonnets with Cathleen on the Norfolk coast during his pre-Christmas leave. The first of the five published under the title *1914* – the book which gave Brooke the experience that, as Byron put it a century before, he "woke up famous" – was called 'Peace'. It included the lines that have since become known as a gratuitous, naive and fatuous glorification of war:

"Now, God be thanked Who has matched us
   with His hour,
 And caught our youth, and wakened us from
   sleeping,
With hand made sure, clear eye, and sharpened
   power,
To turn, as swimmers into cleanness leaping,
Glad from a world grown old and cold and
   weary,
 Leave the sick hearts that honour could not
   move,

And half-men, and their dirty songs and dreary,
    And all the little emptiness of love!"

Leaving aside what Brooke called, rather insultingly for those who still suffered by loving him, "the little emptiness of love", this is a picture he painted of his own feelings about himself and the war. It is true that Brooke reluctantly embraced the war, partly because of his outrage at what he saw in Antwerp, and partly because of the need he had always felt – as a Fabian member – for a cause greater than himself. There is also an element of the bitter shame at the way he had behaved with Ka, Noel and Bryn. There was an uncomplicated inevitability about war which swept him up and simplified the constant nagging questions about what he should do and who he should love.

He expressed something that so many of his contemporaries seem to have felt at the outbreak of war, a mild liberation from the small selfishnesses of their lives so far. There was, though, a side-swipe at the "sick hearts that honour could not move", a reference perhaps to Lytton Strachey and the hated Bloomsbury circle, most of whom were now pacifists.

The last sonnet of the collection, 'The Soldier', was not his favourite but has become one of the most famous in the English language and certainly one of the most famous lines that came out of the First World War. Like the swimmers leaping into cleanness, it has been criticised for glorifying war and military self-sacrifice. But it is more than that. It expresses something of the way he comforted himself at the prospect of his own imminent non-existence and it is, at the same time, an evocation of Englishness by one of the most obviously English poets in the *Oxford Book of English Verse*.

He wrote the first line, "if I should die, think only this of me", in camp on 23 December 1914. By the end of Christmas, it was finished. It caught the spirit of the time. 'The Soldier' is masterful in its construction as a sonnet, though – in comparison with the war poets who were to come – it looks naive and even self-obsessive. But the main theme is the identification with the land of England, something that his friend Edward Thomas clearly understood. "Literally for this," Thomas said, describing why he had decided to enlist, and running soil through his fingers. It was an idea of the land as spiritually and politically vital, an idea borrowed from Brooke's friend Hilaire Belloc, the anti-socialist radical.

After Christmas, Brooke managed to persuade his new friend Violet Asquith to invite him to Walmer Castle on the Kent coast, where the Prime Minister's family was spending the seasonal holiday. "Can you really find room for me among all those field marshals? And may I wear khaki and finish a sonnet?"

It was shortly after this that the fatal letter from Tahiti arrived, revealing that he was by then almost certainly a father. But events at Walmer were coming to a head and would decide his fate. On Boxing Day, two memos had arrived on the desk of Prime Minister Asquith by two of his most intelligent strategic thinkers —Maurice Hankey of the Committee of Imperial Defence and Churchill.

Even before the news of the peculiar Christmas Truce on the western front had filtered back to England, Churchill and Hankey had in their different ways begun to perceive the truth: that the Western Front was now bogged down in stalemate and any attempt to break it would be devastating in human lives. Why, they asked themselves, should Lord Kitchener's new volunteer armies, now under training in England, be wasted by being sent, as Churchill put it, "to chew barbed wire"? Churchill and Hankey agreed that there had to be a better, more humane way to win the war. So began the ultimately ill-fated idea of forcing the Dardanelles to knock Turkey out of the war, to supply Russia and to unite central Europe on the allied side. History condemns it as wrong-headed, and with the benefit of hindsight perhaps it was, but – at the time – it united those humanitarian radicals, mainly in the Liberal Party, who could see what would happen on the Western Front and were desperate for an alternative.

On New Year's Day, still at Walmer Castle, Asquith replied asking Churchill to "put your detailed plans in hand at once". For the rest of the month, Churchill was hammering out the basic strategy for the Dardanelles. Violet Asquith wrote half a century later: "Personal emotion may have burred my vision, but I saw it then and see it still as the most imaginative conception of the First World War, and one which might, had all gone well, have proved the shortest route to victory."

The ultimate tragedy of the Dardanelles, the result of poor leadership and bureaucratic inertia back home which delayed the expedition, meant that the inexorable slaughter of the Western Front had to be played out in all its horror – the great disaster of Western European history. Its failure had wider consequences: Churchill was flung from office, the Liberal Party went the same way, and arguably the Russian Revolution became inevitable.

These momentous events, which would cast a shadow over the rest of the century, were being decided while Brooke was staying at Walmer. Violet Asquith was famously indiscrete, and she was the close personal support of her father, who was also famously indiscrete – he was carrying on a long affair by letter with Venetia Stanley at the time, where his most intimate thoughts and consideration were set down. So Brooke may well have known what was emerging, and it clearly appealed to his continuing romanticism – a military expedition to take Constantinople.

5

The grave

War need never have broken out between Turkey and the allies. The real tension was between Turkey and Russia, but determined German diplomacy had been designed to lure Turkey into the conflict more widely, and the seizure of Turkish ships building in Britain at the outbreak of war heightened the underlying tensions. The German battlecruiser *Goeben* and the light cruiser *Bresslau* had been sent to the Mediterranean in October 1913, and their commander Rear Admiral Wilhelm Souchon turned out to be a brilliant diplomat and a thrower of lavish parties.

The diplomacy in the eastern Mediterranean began to boil over as the final countdown to war accelerated. A secret agreement between Germany and Turkey promised that both would declare war on Russia simultaneously. A secret agreement between the British and French and Russians promised that, if war was to happen, then Constantinople would eventually to the Russians.

On 4 August 1914, Souchon and his squadron was ordered to Constantinople and the British admiral allowed him to escape for fear of pre-empting the declaration of war. The Turks, horrified about what the arrival of a German squadron would mean for their relations with the allies, bought the ships outright and appointed Souchon head of the Turkish navy. War followed at the end of October when Souchon bombarded the Russian Black Sea coast. The British and French declared war early in November.

Since Souchon had disappeared up the Dardanelles, the British Mediterranean Fleet had been waiting at the other end, under the political control of the First Lord of the Admiralty, Winston Churchill. Churchill's bold plan was now to force the Dardanelles by sea, and the fleet would be followed if necessary with a landing by troops – seizing Constantinople and opening a way to re-supply the struggling Russians. But everything depended on speed and the services began dragging their feet. The Russians vetoed the involvement of Greek forces. The First Sea Lord, now the energetic, ancient and difficult Lord Fisher, vacillated back and forth in his support. Slowly – far too slowly – an Anglo-French naval force began to gather on the Greek island of Lemnos, in the windswept natural harbour of Mudros.

Mudros Harbour had been almost unused before but, during the early months of 1915, it began to fill up with an extraordinary array of people and equipment, huts for the soldiers and doctors, makeshift docks and harbour cranes, labourers from Egypt, nurses from Canada, turbaned troops from India, bronzed Anzacs from New Zealand and Australia, huge lines of bell tents and vast Red Cross marquees, French battleships with strange bows sliding into the water, Russian cruisers with five funnels, old steamers disguised as battlecruisers, the huge Atlantic liner *Aquitania* painted white as a hospital ship, and the bleak rocky hills in the background. The Australian doctor Claude Morlet wrote this:

"Nearly all the young women were shipped away from the island on arrival of the troops (which is a mercy). There are now all men, or old hags and children. They are living in villages made of stone and plaster – filthy, untidy and ramshackle. They have some beautiful orchards and plantations, and ride about on donkeys and mules, and herd sheep and goats about the barren hills. As in Egypt, there are no fences. It is however the military aspect of the place that is so interesting. Thousands of troops are camped around the harbour – British, French, Indians, Australians and New Zealanders. Everywhere there is a scene of most frenzied activity – an enormous sense of urgency. Piers and wharves are being made. Roads, bridges, and railways being built. Several thousands of labourers have been brought from Egypt and Malta, and the air is filled with the sounds of hammering, clanking of chains, blasting of rock; shouts and noise of the busy thousands, mixed with bugle calls – and the ever-present distant rumble of the guns!"

New arrivals described the troops standing in silence as they moved slowly into the harbour for the first time, to be greeted with this extraordinary scene. The marines tested out their techniques with an experimental landing at the end of February, and they found themselves unopposed. Confidence was running high: the naval commander-in-chief Sir Sackville Carden reported at the beginning of March that he planned to be in Constantinople within a fortnight. The price of wheat fell on the world markets in response.

But all was not as straightforward as it seemed. The Turkish forces were badly equipped but well-trained and commanded, and were very far from being the pushover the allies were expecting to encounter. They also now had time to prepare for the inevitable landings, laying the new magnetic mines along the Dardanelles in preparation. Carden was also having doubts and was suffering from nervous exhaustion.

Two days before the planned attack by the fleet, Carden went on sick leave, handing over to his deputy, John de Roebeck. The 18 March attack was a disaster. When de Roebeck lost his nerve and tried to turn the fleet, the old battleships under his command ran into the minefield and three were sunk and three more badly damaged. It was the worst British setback at sea since Nelson's day. De Roebeck's chief of staff, Commodore Roger Keyes – later the architect of the Zeebrugge Raid in 1918 – urged him to make an immediate second attempt, and it seems likely at that point that the fleet would have got through. The Turks believed that the British and French had deliberately withheld, so that the Russians should not get Constantinople.

But rather than pressing on or abandoning the whole idea of taking that city, the military planners decided to try again by land. De Roebeck was told to wait until the army was ready. Back in London, Churchill agreed with Keyes, but he was over-ruled by the War Office. No land attack could take place before mid-April.

This was the theatre of war where Brooke was sent. He was briefed, along with the other Royal Naval Division officers at Blandford by their commander Major-General Sir Archibald Paris. They were told that it would be a perilous mission, accompanying the fleet as the spearhead for the attack, and Churchill's plans had always included the RND from the start. Brooke must have known that his chances of survival were at the very least in the balance, and he understood that they would leave for the Mediterranean within six weeks. It was then mid-January. It had only been two weeks since Asquith had told Churchill to proceed with more detailed plans.

Brooke's attitude then a mixture of his new idealism, together with his former cynicism and his continuing horror of old age. "I had hoped that England'ld get on her legs again, achieve youth and merriment, and slough the things I loathe – capitalism and feminism and hermaphroditism and the rest," he wrote to the poet John Drinkwater, trying to shame him into leaving the theatre. "But on mature consideration, pursued over muddy Dorset, I think there'll not be much change ... come and die. It'll be great fun."

On sick leave at the end of January, looked after in Eddie Marsh's flat, he met Churchill again and said that he did not expect to survive the attack. Churchill told him to put his trust in the destructive power of the navy. The remaining weeks in England were spent covered in mud in his exercises, and on one occasion came close to being run over in the pouring rain by a car bearing

Marsh and Churchill's wife Clementine. They sailed at end of February, with only enough equipment for two weeks of fighting. It was a measure partly of the shortage of resources, as Churchill struggled to extract them from the Western Front, but also of the overwhelming optimism.

Violet Asquith came with Clementine Churchill to see them off. Churchill himself was there. So was the King. "It somehow wasn't quite the fun it ought to have been," she wrote. "I had a tightening of the heart throughout." It was tough for Violet. She identified with the Dardanelles escapade, believed in Churchill and the need to avoid the slaughter in France and Belgium.

But the success of the operation was not a matter of theory for her. Her closest friends, and her brother Oc, were all involved and their very lives probably now depended on its success. All were also now in Hood Battalion. Hood marched to the train and arrived at Avonmouth, where they boarded the Union Castle liner *Grantully Castle*. Violet followed by car and sent a final love letter to Brooke on board. He stayed away from the ship's side during the final farewell. According to

Virginia Woolf later, Violet said in 1916 that she had loved Brooke "as she had never loved any man".

On board, Brooke wrote a final a letter to Marsh to be opened in the event of his death. He asked him to clean up his letters, destroying anything from Elisabeth van Rysselberghe and Eileen Wellesley, and giving him an address in Tahiti for Taatamata so that she could be told of his death.

The *Grantully Castle*, Brooke's home now for the rest of his life, arrived in Malta on 8 March. "Death might be an admirable solution," he wrote to Marsh. It was an admission that the exhausting indecision of his love life, and his own sense of unworthiness, seemed to make dying on active service the simplest option.

It was a symptom of the international nature of the disaster which was beginning to unfold that so many troops from all over the world were now gathering in Lemnos: Indians, Anzacs, British marines, French North Africans, their equipment mixed up between decks of the liners which brought them to these Greek islands, with little or no planning about what could possibly bind them together. "They went like kings in a pageant to the imminent death," wrote Brooke's friend John Masefield, then at Mudros with the Red Cross.

It was partly because of this, and partly to have space to sort themselves out, that the RND departed almost immediately for Egypt. There, Brooke, Oc Asquith and Patrick Shaw-Stewart went ashore on a trip to Cairo, where they met Aubrey Herbert, the diplomat and future MP, who was on the staff of Lieutenant-General Sir William Birdwood. They pretended they had been practicing their only Turkish sentence: 'Do not kill me – I am a friend of Herbert Effendi."

It was hardly surprising that the friends in Hood were in a classical frame of mind. They began to call themselves the Argonauts, after Jason, who had plied these waters before them. The diplomat Charles Lister was a new addition to the Argonauts, and it was he who led the parodies of the divisional orders that were emerging from the allied high command, especially the ludicrous one about the vulnerability of the Turkish soldiers to night attack because they were afraid of the dark – "Turks as a rule do not in ordinary times of peace sleep without a light burning," it said – a prime example of the military mind deluding itself.   Brooke had been ill in the New Year and had never fully recovered. Now he was feeling in reduced health again, suffering from sunstroke and diarrhoea. A diet of arrowroot doesn't build up a propensity for violence, he wrote. "I am as weak as a pacifist." But he insisted on getting up from his sickbed to take part in the inspection by the commander-in-chief, Sir Ian Hamilton.

Hamilton also wrote poems. "A notable meeting," Brooke boasted to Violet. "Our greatest poet-soldier ad our greatest soldier-poet. We talked blank verse. He looked very worn and white-haired. I thought him a little fearful – not fearful, but less than cock-sure – about the job."

Like Carden a few weeks before, Hamilton was indeed becoming aware of the overwhelming difficulties ahead. The meeting with Brooke was also a sign of his sudden fame. Hamilton took Hood's colonel aside. "Mind you take care of him," he said. "His loss would be a national loss."

In fact, the fatal mosquito had already done its damage.

Sailing back to Mudros Harbour in the *Grantully Castle*, Brooke was now sharing a cabin with the only American member of the Argonauts, the future stockbroker Johnny Dodge, who painted the cabin walls in fluorescent paint. They arrived on 17 April, to find the harbour packed with 200 ships of all shapes and sizes. They moved on to the island of Skyros.

Brooke was still unwell, lying in his bunk for much of the time, planning what he called a 'threnody for England', running through his head. It was cold and the allied commanders were finding that communication across the hugely diverse forces available to them was extremely difficult. Hamilton was criticised afterwards for heading off with his closest aides to the flagship, the battleship *Queen Elizabeth*. It made sense to co-ordinate closely with the navy, but his own operational staff were on another ship.

He also later failed to take advantage of that position too, even though he could see – from the quarter deck of the flagship – how a new landing on Y Beach could have outflanked the defending Turks, because he said he didn't want to interfere with his commanders on the ground.

Other planning was threadbare. The surgeon-general and other military chiefs had now arrived and were appalled at how little was in place. There were only two old hospital ships and no field hospitals ready. Military commanders, as so often before a military disaster, were hampered also their vast depth of ignorance about the Turks, under their German commanders, and their fatal under-estimation of their fighting ability. "I did not know, to tell you the truth, that they were nearly as good as they turned out to be," Hamilton told the Dardanelles inquiry later.

Brooke and his colleagues were ordered to test their mettle and land on Skyros – officially Turkish soil – as if it was the invasion. They scurried ashore in boats and then raced back again. Freyberg beat Asquith swimming back to the ship. "The sight of one's own men lying down in line among the stones and scrub of these jolly hills charms the blood," wrote Charles Lister. "I hope I shall be brave; I am sure they will."

On 21 April, Oc Asquith wrote to Violet that Rupert had fallen ill again, with a swollen lip, a temperature of 101 and pains in the back and head. Clegg Kelly looked into his cabin before breakfast the following day, and "found him very dazed, but I had no idea he was dangerously ill". On 22 April, he was finally diagnosed with blood poisoning and the medical staff on board *Grantully Castle* were concerned. Without antibiotics, blood poisoning was potentially fatal. The battalion doctor decided to move him to the French hospital ship *Duguay-Trouin*, moored nearby. His fellow Argonauts Asquith and Denis Browne lowered him over the side and into a steam pinnance.

There was no improvement and it was becoming clear that the worst was inevitable. Asquith and Browne stayed on board the *Duguay-Trouin* for the rest of the day but left at 6pm to find General Paris' headquarters so that he could warn Churchill and Hamilton that Rupert would probably die.

The following day was St George's Day, the English national day. Brooke was now unconscious. "At least twice when I spoke to him, he seemed to make an effort in his throat to speak but no words came," said Asquith later. At 2pm, he was relieved by Browne and went to make arrangements for the funeral. He managed to get hold of a solid oak coffin from the ship's store and a cauterising iron, with which he burned Brooke's name and the date on the lid.

Rather more than two hours later, Rupert Brooke died. It was 4.46pm – Browne noted the time – and he had not regained consciousness. The sun was shining all round his cabin, and "the cool sea breeze blowing through the door and shaded windows," he wrote later. "No one could have wished a quieter or calmer end than in that lovely bay, shielded by the mountains and fragrant with sage and thyme."

The Argonauts gathered that evening in an olive grove high above Trebuki Bay on Skyros – Browne, Freyberg, Lister, Kelly, Shaw-Stewart, Asquith and Johnny Dodge. By 8.15pm, General Paris and his staff had arrived, together with the coffin – covered in a union flag – carried by stokers from the RND, lit by a flickering lantern, and accompanied by a French guard of honour.

By 10.45pm, they had reached the graveside. The RND chaplain read the burial service by the light from flaming torches. Asquith saw the grave was too short for the coffin, leapt in and lengthened it with a spade. He found it was

already lined with olive and sage. Shaw-Stewart
led a firing party firing a salvo over the grave, and
a trumpeter from Hood battalion played the Last
Post. Everyone left, except Asquith, Kelly,
Freyberg, Lister and Browne, who stayed talking
in the moonlight, looking for pebbles and bits of
amber to lay on the grave.

Their Greek interpreter had written on the back
of the bigger of the two crosses: 'Here lies the
servant of God, a sub-lieutenant in the English
navy, who died for the deliverance of
Constantinople from the Turks." It was the kind of
romantic epitaph Brooke would have appreciated.

The landings had originally been set for that very
day, 23 April, but they had been postponed for 48
hours because of bad weather. All that day, when
Brooke was struggling between life and death,
with the poison in his veins, the troop transports
and borrowed liners had been raising steam in
Mudros and the other temporary anchorages in
the islands. Four hours after the burial party had
returned to the *Grantully Castle*, the invasion fleet
sailed.

It was a thrilling moment in the early dawn light, as one by one the ships proceeded to sea with the troops roaring from the sides and the military bands playing. By the evening of 24 April, more than two hundred ships were steaming across the Aegean, with Hood battalion heading for a diversionary attack in the Gulf of Saros. By the early hours of Sunday 25 April, they were lying offshore. The troops were woken, given a hot meal and sent to the boats.

By now the world knew, not only that the invasion was under way but that Rupert Brooke was dead. Early reports suggested that he had died of sunstroke. The news had been passed to Hamilton on the evening that he died. "Death grins at my elbow," he wrote in his diary:

"I cannot get him out of my thoughts. He is fed up with the old and sick – only the flower of the flock will serve him now, for God has started a celestial spring cleaning, and our star is to be scrubbed bright with the blood of our bravest and our best."

Violet Asquith was staying at the Viceregal

Lodge in Dublin when she heard the news, and sobbed for hours. She claimed later that it was her greatest sorrow of the war – "and one of the greatest of my life."

"My darling," he father, the prime minister, wrote to his intimate confidante Venetia Stanley the night the news came through. "I can't tell you what I feel about Rupert Brooke's death. It has given me more pain than any loss in the war. We have seen a good deal of him all this autumn & winter, he and Oc being fellow officers, & the closest companions & friends. And Violet & he had a real friendship – perhaps the germ at any rate (as I once said to you) of something more. He was clean-cut & beautiful to look at, and had a streak of something more than talent; his Sonnets struck a fine note. Altogether, by *far* the most attractive & winning of the younger men whom I have got to know since the war began..."

Searching through Brooke's belongings on the way to Gallipoli, his friends found the letter he had written to Eddie Marsh: "You must decide everything about publication. Don't print much bad stuff. Give my love to the *New Numbers* folk, and Violet and Masefield and a few who'd like it."

As an afterthought, he had added: "Get Cathleen anything she wants."

The feint attack involving Hood was brief and perilous, at least for Freyberg, who volunteered to swim ashore and light a beacon. The poor planning and fatal delays had doomed Hamilton's attack, with the most terrible consequences for those taking part on both sides. The slaughter was all the worse because Hamilton made the opposite mistake to Admiral de Roebeck in the first attempt to force the narrows: he would not give up, despite the obvious conclusion that the whole conception was flawed.

Denis Browne passed Skyros on way back towards the fighting, with the rest of Hood, on 2 June. He wrote:

"We passed Rupert's island at sunset. The sea and sky in the east were grey and misty, but it stood out in the west, black and immense, with a crimson glowing halo around it. Every colour had come into the sea and sky to do him honour, and it seemed that the island must ever be shining with his glory that we buried him there."

Two days later, Browne was dead, killed when he and his comrades were flung into the front line in the Third Battle of Krithia. His body was never found. "I've gone now too," he wrote in a final letter to Eddie Marsh found after his death. "Not too badly I hope. I'm luckier than Rupert, because I've fought. But there's no one to bury me as I buried him, so perhaps he's best off in the long run. I got a little image from a tomb for you at Cairo: will you ask my mother for it? It is with the rest of my things, packed in a cigarette box. Dent is looking after my MS music. Good-bye, my dear, & bless you always for your goodness to me. W.D.B."

Back in London, the self-appointed creator of the myth of Rupert Brooke was Churchill himself, signing his obituary in the *Times* as 'WSC':

"The thoughts to which he gave expression in the very few incomparable war sonnets which he has left behind will be shared by many thousands of young men moving resolutely and blithely forward into this, the hardest, cruellest, and the least-rewarded of all the wars that men have fought. They are a whole history and revelation of Rupert Brooke himself. Joyous, fearless, versatile, deeply instructed, with classic symmetry of mind and body, he was all that one would wish England's noblest sons to be in days when no sacrifice but the most precious is acceptable, and the most precious is that which is most freely proffered."

The idea of 'precious sacrifice...freely proffered" sticks in the throat for a modern reader, but these were the elements combined in their final form – "all that one would wish England's noblest sons to be". It was a reputation that Brooke's mother, and then his self-appointed literary executors – led by Geoffrey Keynes – defended with all their might for most of the rest of the century. There was a hint that Brooke had been, not the confused, prudish, occasionally brutal, above all flawed young man, but a demigod – perfect in body and mind – who sacrificed himself. "It must always be a satisfaction for Rupert Brooke's admirers," wrote the *Sunday Times* in June 1915 – with the blood still spilling in Gallipoli, "that he rose to the occasion, answered the call of the hour no less in his poetry – the 1914 sonnets – as in practical service of his country."

But this was a nation at war, suffering the most appalling casualties and holding together at a cost that has echoed down the decades since. This was a moment in national history when heroes were required, and it helped if they were soldiers. Bizarrely, the man hailed by the *Times* as Brooke's successor was his friend Arthur 'Oc' Asquith, whose own slim volume came out at the end of 1915. It included some strange verses about a baby paddling near the front lines:

> "Hail, Oh baby of the May,
> In the bubbling river-bed,
> Playing where the cannon play
> With the shrapnel overhead."

6

Afterword

Brooke's tomb was repaired by the British in 1931, and a naked statue was erected nearby on Skyros to celebrate him. Three decades later, in 1961, the destroyer HMS *Saintes* was sent from Malta to restore the grave. Three years later, the approved biography appeared by Ivor Novello's librettist Christopher Hassall. It was more than three decades before the historian Nigel Jones pieced together some of the clues and the letters pointing to the truth, Brooke's breakdown, his child in Tahiti and his extraordinary and agonising ability to juggle rival affairs simultaneously.

But there was a revealing review of Hassall's book when it appeared, by the historian Philip Toynbee, whose wife had known Brooke well. He complained that the book had painted a picture of an "insufferable poseur". There was certainly that element about Brooke's character as a young man.

But Toynbee went on to compare Brooke with his near contemporary T. E. Lawrence, both tortured by prudery and indecision, both taken up by the same glittering Liberal circles, both "tormented neurotics", both "brave egotists":

"Both Lawrence and Brooke tried as hard as they could to escape the really dreadful apparatus of enthroned mediocrity and bejewelled vulgarity which was the English ruling class in its last phase of unself-questioning authority. I believe that neither of them succeeded in escaping."

This is, of course, only half true. Brooke never tried very hard to escape his friendship with Violet Asquith, nor his affair with Eileen Wellesley, though perhaps he might have done if he had lived. But Toynbee's comments are fascinating because they allow us to wonder what Brooke's life would have been like if he had survived the war. This is unanswerable, but it might be possible to set the question more clearly.

Virginia Woolf certainly believed that, had he returned from the Dardanelles, he would have been a prominent Labour politician, perhaps – though she did not see it herself – in the Labour cabinet of 1945, alongside his friend Hugh Dalton.

He certainly might have returned to his original Fabian loyalties, but Brooke seemed to have put aside Fabianism – which he was anyway juggling with the more populist, more extreme English alternatives. Whose side was he on in the famous debate where he cut Noel Olivier, between Shaw and Belloc? We don't really know. But his extraordinary ability to create a loyal, not to say fanatically uncritical following, does point towards some kind of political career. It is certainly possible that he would have come back so intertwined with the Asquith family, and have married Violet – as she and her father both hoped he would – and have become the powerhouse of her lonely political crusade for her father, and after that for Edwardian Liberalism against the corporatism and cronyism of Lloyd George.

But even that hardly rings quite true. If Brooke had escaped not just the Dardanelles but also the Western Front, and also – unlike Oc Asquith – escaped promotion to general at a frighteningly early age, he would have come back to face his war sonnets in the light of four years of slaughter, no longer quite like the "swimmers into cleanness leaping".

Perhaps Toynbee was right, and Brooke would have followed Lawrence of Arabia into a tortured, embittered seclusion.

Further reading

I am indebted to Nigel Jones' excellent, definitive and witty biography of Brooke (see below), which brought his subject alive in three dimensions for the first time and must be a first stop for anyone who wants to know more.. I have also relied on:

H. H. Asquith (1982) *Letters to Venetia Stanley*, ed. Michael and Eleanor Brock, Oxford: OUP.

Violet Bonham Carter (1967) *Winston Churchill As I Knew Him*, 2nd edition, London: Pan.

Rupert Brooke (1928) *The Collected Poems of Rupert Brooke*, memoir by Edward Marsh, London: Sidgwick & Jackson.

Rupert Brooke (1947) *The Poetical Works of Rupert Brooke*, ed. Geoffrey Keynes, London:

Faber & Faber.

Rupert Brooke (1987) *The Collected Poems of Rupert Brooke*, introduction by Gavin Ewart, London, Faber & Faber

Colin Clifford (2002) The Asquiths, London: John Murray.

Christopher Hassall (1964) *Rupert Brooke: A Biography*, London: Faber & Faber.

Michael Hastings (1967) *The Handsomest Young Man in England,* London: Michael Joseph.

Nigel Jones (2003), *Rupert Brooke: Life, Death and Myth*, 2nd edition, London: BBC Books.

Geoffrey Keynes (1981) *The Gates of Memory*, Oxford: OUP

John Lehmann (1980) *Rupert Brooke: his Life and his Legend*, London: Quartet.

Cathleen Nesbitt (1975) *A Little Love and Good*

Company, London: Faber & Faber.

Christopher Page (1999) *Command in the Royal Naval Division: A military biography of Brigadier A. M. Asquith,* Staplehurst: Spellmount.

Gwen Raverat (1952), *Period Piece*, London: Faber & Faber.

Mike Read (1998) *Forever England*, London: Mainstream.

By the same author...

Unheard, Unseen: Submarine E14 and the Dardanelles

The Dardanelles in the early hours of 27 April 1915. Here Agamemnon and the Greeks landed for the attack on Troy. Here Xerxes had ordered the sea to be lashed for destroying his invasion bridges. Here Lord Byron swam against the Hellespont current.

Now it was the very portals of the Ottoman Empire for the crew of the British submarine E14, staring silently into the darkness from the small conning tower, eight feet above the waves. It meant mines, forts, searchlights and wire s ubmarine nets. It meant a formidable current pouring fresh water over strange and unpredictable layers of salt water up the 38 mile passage from the Mediterranean to the Sea of

Marmora, and through one narrow point only three quarters of a mile wide. It meant undertaking possibly the longest dive ever contemplated in a submarine.

It also meant passing the wreckage of the submarines that had tried to pass that way in the days and weeks before, the French submarine *Saphir* and the British E15, lying wrecked and battered on a sandbank off Kephez Point, their dead buried on the beach, their survivors in captivity.

The sea was absolutely smooth and there was only a breath of air from the movement of the submarine itself. The canvas screens around the bridge had been removed to make the conning tower less visible. The electric batteries that would power their motors underwater had been charged to their highest pitch, as they waited in their harbour of Tenedos with its medieval castle, its windmills and its Greek sailing *caiques*, just a few miles from the site of ancient Troy.

E14 had weighed anchor at 1.40 in the morning. There was no escort for their lonely voyage. The goodbyes had been said. They had written their farewell letters, knowing that the chances were now against their survival, and given them into safekeeping.

The submarine's captain, Lieutenant Commander Courtney Boyle, had written three – to his wife, his parents and his solicitor – in the three hours warning he had been given at Mudros harbour the day before. Now he stood in his navy greatcoat, holding onto the rail, his binoculars around his neck, staring ahead in the blackness at the navigation lights of the allied warships, the greens and reds slipping away behind him. Next to him, his navigating officer, Lieutenant Reginald Lawrence, only 22 years old, a reserve officer from the merchant navy, who had been there just a year before in peacetime. Below, the executive officer, Edward Stanley, was supervising the control room, listening to the rhythmic pulse of the engines.

It was a flat calm and there was no moon. From the northern shore in the distance ahead of them came the boom of guns and the flash of high explosive, a reminder that British, Australian, New Zealand and Indian troops were now dug in on the beaches, after their dramatic and perilous landings 48 hours before. Closer to the invasion beaches, they could see the shimmer of tiny glows from the trenches, the cigarette ends and makeshift fires of the soldiers dug into the dunes.

On their left hand side, there was a huge searchlight by the Suan Dere river; Boyle's first objective was to get as close as possible to the estuary there before diving. Beyond that, he could see searchlights on both shores, sweeping the sea ahead of them. He and Lawrence reckoned the one past the white cliffs on the southern shore must be Kephez Point, where E15 had come to grief and, further ahead, a more powerful yellow light, was the great fort at Chanak.

One diesel engine drove them ahead, and the noise and the fumes were horribly apparent to anyone on the conning tower, where the exhaust pipe was. Boyle was as experienced a submarine commander as any other afloat, but he was aware that he had not quite earned his commander's confidence. The calculations about speed, battery endurance, current and all the rest had been going through his head constantly since the dramatic meeting in the fleet flagship just two weeks before when– like all but one in the room – he had judged the venture impossible. That single dissenting voice was now dead.

He was aware also that, if the commander of E15 had not declared the passage of the Dardanelles possible by submarine, then almost certainly – as the most senior commander present – he would have been asked to try anyway. The one ray of hope was that the Australian submarine AE2, under the command of Henry Stoker, had now signalled that they had got through. This news had reached the E14 immediately before their departure and had changed the mood of the crew from resigned acceptance to hopeful elation. The passage of the Dardanelles must be possible after all, even if it remained extraordinarily hazardous.

But Boyle did have a plan. It was to get as far as possible to conserve their battery before diving, to dive as deep as possible under the obstructions, but to rise to periscope depth as often as possible in the most difficult sections of the journey, where the current was most unpredictable, to make sure the submarine did not drift   He was acutely aware that his own skill and experience was now the determining factor, above all others, in his survival, the survival of the other 29 men on board, and of course of the success or otherwise of the mission. They passed a brightly lit hospital ship, with its red crosses illuminated under spotlights, and then they were alone at the mouth of the Dardanelles.

The crew were sent below and the engine room hatch was closed as a precaution. The Suan Dere searchlight loomed ahead, swept over them and then came back. Had they been seen? It flashed away again. It was clear from the experience of the ancient trawlers the British were using as minesweepers that the batteries ignored small ships on the way up the Dardanelles, waiting for them to drift closer to the shore as they turned back before firing. It was not clear either how much the stripped down conning tower was visible.

Then the searchlight was back and this time it stayed on them for 30 seconds. Lawrence gave a strained laugh. They had been seen. Boyle sent Lawrence below and ordered diving stations. By the time the hatch had been shut behind them, and they had swept down the iron ladder into the control room, two shots been fired. Lawrence settled down with his notebook in the control room. "Now we had really started on our long dive," he wrote later.

Everything now depended on the captain's skill and the resources of their electric batteries to drive them underwater....

Read more: *Unheard, Unseen* available from Amazon on Kindle and in paperback.

Other titles by David Boyle

Building Futures
Funny Money: In search of alternative cash
What is New Economics?
The Sum of our Discontent
The Tyranny of Numbers
The Money Changers
Numbers (with Anita Roddick)
Authenticity: Brands, Fakes, Spin and the Lust for
Real Life
Blondel's Song
Leaves the World to Darkness (fiction)
News from Somewhere (*editor*)
Toward the Setting Sun
The New Economics: A Bigger Picture (with
Andrew Simms)
Money Matters: Putting the eco into economics
The Wizard
The Little Money Book
Why London Needs its own Currency
Eminent Corporations (with Andrew Simms)
Voyages of Discovery
The Human Element
On the Eighth Day, God Created Allotments
The Age to Come
What if money grew on trees (*editor*)

Unheard, Unseen: Submarine E14 and the Dardanelles
Broke: How to survive the middle class crisis
Alan Turing: Unlocking the Enigma
Peace on Earth: The Christmas truce of 1914
Jerusalem: England's National Anthem
Give and Take (with Sarah Bird)
People Powered Prosperity (with Tony Greenham)
Rupert Brooke: England's Last Patriot
How to be English
Operation Primrose
Before Enigma
The Piper (fiction)
Scandal
How to become a freelance writer
Regicide (fiction)
Cancelled!
The Death of Liberal Democracy (with Joe Zammit-Lucia)
V for Victory

See also our website at www.therealpress.couk

Made in the USA
Lexington, KY
09 August 2017